TO

_____

FROM

_____

RUMI
BRIDGE TO THE SOUL

RUMI
BRIDGE TO THE SOUL

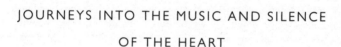

JOURNEYS INTO THE MUSIC AND SILENCE
OF THE HEART

Translations by Coleman Barks,
with A. J. Arberry and Nevit Ergin

HarperOne
An Imprint of HarperCollins*Publishers*

PHOTO CREDITS

p. 2: Ali Mazerheri; p. 3: Ali Mazerheri; p. 6: Farid Mohammadi;
p. 7: From *A Survey of Persian Art: From Prehistoric Times to the Present*,
volume III, Architecture, Arthur Upham Pope, editor (SOPA, ASHIYA, 1981);
p. 14: Farid Mohammadi; p. 16: Farid Mohammadi;
p. 17: Farid Mohammadi; p. 19: Carl Marcus; p. 23: Farid Mohammadi

HarperOne

HarperCollins books may be purchased for educational, business,
or sales promotional use. For information please write: Special Markets
Department, HarperCollins Publishers, 10 East 53rd Street,
New York, NY 10022.

HarperCollins Web site: http://www.harpercollins.com

HarperCollins®, 📖®, and HarperOne™
are trademarks of HarperCollins Publishers.

Library of Congress Cataloging-in-Publication Data is available.

ISBN: 978-0-06-133816-8
ISBN-10: 0-06-133816-8

09 10 11 RRD (H) 10 9 8 7 6

For Robert Bly

Contents

Introduction

    BRIDGE, POEM, AWARENESS MOVING THROUGH   1

    TRAVEL NOTES   13

The Poems

  1. A BOWL FALLEN FROM THE ROOF   27

  2. A STORY THEY KNOW   28

  3. HARVEST   29

  4. INHALE AUTUMN, LONG FOR SPRING   30

  5. LEAVES ABOUT TO LET GO   32

  6. A LIGHT WITHIN HIS LIGHT   34

  7. A KING DRESSED AS A SERVANT   36

  8. AS THE SKY DOES IN WATER   37

  9. THE TIME OF DIVULGING   38

  10. EMPTY   41

  11. NICKNAMES   42

  12. NEW BLOSSOMS   43

  13. SPLIT THE SACK   44

  14. ANY SPRIG OF AN HERB   46

  15. SECRET PLACES   48

  16. DOORSILL   49

  17. FLIGHTPATHS   50

  18. MUSIC AND SILENCE   51

  19. EARSIGHT   52

  20. THE TALKING   53

  21. CURRENCY   54

  22. WATER FROM THE WELL OF THE SOUL   56

23. ANOTHER INVITATION   57

24. THE ONE WHO LEFT   58

25. DISCIPLINES   59

26. PIECES OF A BROKEN CUP   60

27. SPILLED SPEECH   62

28. SOUL HOUSES   64

29. THE WAVE OF THAT AGREEMENT   66

30. CALM IN THE MIDST OF LIGHTNING   67

31. AVALANCHE   68

32. PURE SILENCE   69

33. WHAT FEAR OF LOSS   70

34. A MOUNTAIN NEST   71

35. MILES OF RIVERSIDE CANEBED   72

36. SOLOMON AND THE WIND OF SPEAKING   74

37. A MIXED-BREED APPLE   75

38. NO EXPECTATIONS   76

39. MOUNTAINTOP TROUGH   78

40. WHAT YOU GAVE   80

41. YOUR TURN AT DICE   81

42. HOLIDAY WITHOUT LIMITS   82

43. OUTDOORS AND THE PASSION OF THE GRASS   84

44. A PREPOSTEROUS GUESS   86

45. ASLEEP AND LISTENING   87

46. PEARL   88

47. GREEN WRIT   89

48. LOOK AT A FOUNTAIN   90

49. DESOLATION   91

50. THE DANCE OF YOUR HIDDEN LIFE   92

51. LET THE SOUP SIMMER   94

52. THE ONLY OBLIGATION   95

53. BUTCHER AND SHEEP   96

54. I SEE THE FACE   97

55. THE MEETING   98

56. THE LIVING DOUBLENESS   100

57. THE VALUE OF THIS MOMENT   102

58. OCEAN LIGHT   103

59. LIKE A FIG   104

60. GONE FOR GOOD   105

61. TWO LOVINGS   106

62. TALKING TO THE LUCK-BIRD   107

63. ALIVE WITH SCRIPTURE   108

64. FAINT LAMENT OF FORM   110

65. THIS HIGH MEADOW   112

66. GRANTED   114

67. SALADIN'S LEAVING   116

68. WHAT YOU HAVE DESPISED IN YOURSELF   117

69. WINTER OR SUMMER   118

70. ABRAHAM AND ISAAC   120

71. I ASK ONE MORE THING   122

72. SEEDS AND RAIN   124

73. ONE BEING INSIDE ALL   125

74. STRUCK TENT   126

75. OPEN WINDOW   127

76. FULL SUN   128

77. I ROCKED MY OWN CHEST   129

78. YOU SHALL NOT SEE ME   130

79. A BEAUTIFUL WALK INSIDE YOU   132

80. LEAVING   134

81. ENERGY YOU CAN SPEND   136

82. ONE THING I DID WRONG   138

83. A NORTHERN WIND   139

84. MIDNIGHT AND SUNRISE   140

85. THE CREATION WORD   141

86. WE ARE THE SUN   142

87. YOU MAKE YOUR OWN OIL AS YOU COOK   143

88. A HUNDRED AND ONE   144

89. WE CANNOT DECIDE   145

90. A WAKING TOWN   146

References   147

Introduction

BRIDGE, POEM, AWARENESS MOVING THROUGH

Rumi's place in the history of religions is as a bridge between faiths. The story of his funeral in 1273 is well known. Representatives came from every religion—Muslims, Christians, Jews, Buddhists, Hindus. When questioned about this, they responded, "He deepens us wherever we are." Rumi lives in the heart, the core (he might call it friendship) of our impulse to praise, to worship, to explore the mystery of union. Even his name is a bridge word.*

But his meeting with Shams Tabriz is the key to his inclusivity. Shams operated beyond form and doctrine. He once said that if the Kaaba were suddenly lifted up out of the world, we would see that each person is really bowing (five times a day) to *every other person*. In other words, if the icons of religions could dissolve, we would be left with the radiance of each other, the one honoring the other as the same glory. Friendship. *Namaste.*

My Love for Bridges

I sometimes fall in love with bridges. One lazy spring when I was staying in a house in Kanlica, across from Istanbul, it was the Sultan Mehmet Bridge, with its Bosphoric procession of boats. The Clifton Suspension Bridge near Bristol, England. The lowly San Mateo Bridge across San Francisco Bay, and all those others across that body of water. The rickety old Walnut Street Bridge we drove over every morning going to elementary

---

* *Rum* refers to the Roman-influenced part of the Anatolian peninsula, roughly everything east of Iconium (Konya), and sometimes, more specifically, to Byzantium, that ultimate bridge city between East and West. In the early thirteenth century the region around Konya was established as the sultanate of Rum by a branch of the Seljuks. *Rum-i* means someone from Konya.

school in Chattanooga. I used to imagine places to live in lodged among the girders, or especially, not on that bridge but others, in the drawbridge lift operator's room. So I was psychically primed for the Khajou Bridge in Isphahan.

Rumi says:

Lovers find secret places
inside this violent world
where they make transactions
with beauty.

#15, SECRET PLACES

The Khajou Bridge during daylight.

Isphahan is world famous for its bridges, but the Khajou Bridge is different from the others in style and decoration, and in the feel of it. The tiled plaques above each alcove have lovely variations. Khajou is a honeycomb of secret places, many of them out in the open, but perfectly suited for any transaction with beauty. The Khajou Bridge over the Zanayeh River in Isphahan is a vision of what a community made of such loverly nooks might look like. It is an encouragement for those sojourning through to rest awhile and deepen. Tarrying is the specialty of the Khajou Bridge. Whitman's "I loafe and invite my soul" was written two centuries after this bridge took form, but it might serve as its motto. Surely no one uses this bridge just to get somewhere. It is as intricate and woven as a brain, a halved and opened labyrinth. The right brain is dominant here, with its artistic sensitivity and wisdom flow, but Khajou is also an image of balance, with its upper roadway, very practical and left-brain, and its lower level conducive to music and meditation, friendship and poetry.

On the downriver side of the high-walled upper road (see the photo below) is an arcade of rooms each capable of holding eight to ten people. Poets in recitation, philosophers arguing, family reunions, the various uses human beings might devise for the evening hours. There are octagonal pavilions on either end and a larger octagon in the center for music. At one time there may have been smaller temporary pavilions on the roof of the central space.

The upper level of the Khajou Bridge.

An early Sufi, Ghazzali, says of the deep listening practice Sufis call *sema:*

When their spirits receive mystical apprehension of the unseen states and their hearts are softened by the lights of divine essence, they sit down, and he who chants, chants a light chant to bring them forth by degrees from the internal to the external.

Water music is the light chant here that brings forth soul.

The Khajou Bridge suggests we try more contemplative ways. Grotto, idyllic bench, sound studio, dissolving mirror, incubation. Our feet dangle off the benches. We relax into childhood and mature grief at once. Singers in these chambers need no audience, though they have one, scattered and deeply engaged. This bridge is a generous moment.

Hart Crane's vision of the Brooklyn Bridge is as a

harp and altar, of the fury fused,
(How could mere toil align thy choiring strings!)....

We have seen night lifted in thine arms.

Crane's prayer to it is for it to

Unto us lowliest sometime sweep, descend
And out of the curveship lend a myth to God.

Khajou Bridge might be that descent. On its lower level it holds its walkers only a few feet over the water. A legend persists that the concrete of this bridge was made of limestone mixed with egg white, like a cake. This bridge was alchemically cooked, a free-for-all *present*. The history of experimentation with various formulae for concrete coincides, of course, with the human building of domes, arches, roads, and especially bridges, aqueducts, and canals. Any structure made to be in water for centuries must have a special stickum in it. Why egg white, I do not know. Any guesses, out there in radioland? This seventeenth-century alchemical mystery is more playful than our national monument, the imposing brickwork that walks us over to Brooklyn. Khajou revels in its sixteen watercourses, with their close-by, right down *in* the water, divinely *human* music. Plato says that music is the knowledge of that which relates to love in harmony and system. Khajou is a chrysalis, a conjugation for the verbs *to flow* and *to flower*. Like Whitman's Brooklyn Ferry this bridge is a crossover where we discover the spiked halo around our heads reflecting in the river as we lean over the railing. But there are no railings here. Khajou is everywhere open and pointed.

Nietzsche says, "What is great in man is that he is a bridge, and not a goal." A human being is a going-across. Khajou is an invitation to the glory of more ordinary activity. Playfulness, stories, inner quiet. It is full of resting-spot compartments. Here is a metaphor to explore. Say the stanzas of a Rumi *ghazal* (ode) have the brio and lively dynamic of the sluices and alcoves of the Khajou Bridge, that they provide spaces where conversation can flourish, and silence, the deep silence we remember near water. I was impressed by the depth of solitude in those who were sitting on the steps looking downstream. The arts of poetry and music and architecture were much more closely woven in Persia in the seventeenth century than they are for us now. So say a Rumi poem is a bridge to the heart, and though the heart is a thronging caravanserai, it is not the ultimate place to live. Nor is a bridge. Pure being is that, or *just* being. Poetry points and persuades us there. Close, but not the place itself. Mystical poetry wants the full consciousness that is beyond words.

Nietzsche once imagined an eighty-thousand-year-old man whose character is *totally alterable,* who can contain an *abundance of different individuals.* This malleable identity easily finds a seat on Khajou and in the ghazals of Rumi. Between a beginningless beginning and an endless end, each of us is a bridge rhythm in time. A dam, a dance, a narrowing of mountain snow-melt before it is allowed to quicken and continue. A conversational music, an echoing bench with old men laughing and talking.

Great architectural forms like cathedrals and mosques, precarious Himalayan monasteries, standing stonehenges, inviting amphitheaters, and pyramids all reveal longings in the human soul, the ways it loves to express itself and simply *be,* under open sky, near a river, against a cliff. It may be naïve to say so, but architectures speak of the joy the soul is here for. If I lived in Isphahan, I would go to the Khajou Bridge several times a week, at different times of day. I was told that there are people known as *bridgemasters,* who understand the soul-growth messages embedded like hidden gems by Khajou's seventeenth-century Sufi architects. I did not meet anyone who admitted to being a bridgemaster, but I did ask around, and I am still looking.

On the matter of this bridge, I am the rankest amateur. I was only on it for part of an evening in May. I did not even *see* the upper level, with

The Khajou Bridge at night.

its road and alcoves. But even with such short acquaintance I feel how the bridge was made to delight in several possibilities of being alive. The same can be said of Rumi's poetry. Likewise, there is a bare openness, almost a danger, about walking out on the wet surfaces of the Khajou Bridge at night. A similar nakedness lives in Rumi's poetry, something not reasonable, a being drawn through/toward surrender.

At night, the Khajou Bridge holds lighted niches and watersound together, an auditory and visual multiplicity within unity. The bridge contains several layers of human interaction, which are not concealed from each other. The Khajou Bridge and the ghazals of Rumi are similar expressions of awareness, a commonplace where we rest *within* restlessness. Bridges work with what flows through and away. The sound of a river running mixes like egg white with the talking, the song, of people passing across. A Rumi poem may be experienced as a series of compartments we inhabit while awash with what moves through us, luminous gold bits. In one of the alcove chambers a man is singing a Hafez poem, grieving, panning for the one not of this world who lives inside these bodies for a time. The Khajou Bridge is a humanmade shoal that people are drawn to, to enjoy the seasonal motion, to sit quietly in time. It is not a tavern, nor is it a school.

The central golden rectangle of Isphahan, the *maidan,* is laid out on a north-south axis, with the main mosque set at an angle to it, its axis aligned with Mecca. The symbolism is clear. Government and business are on one axis, worship on another, profoundly melded, welded, to one another, but at an angle, like a bowing figure. The centerline of the Khajou Bridge casts a vector between the two minaret verticals of the mosque. So Khajou is a call to prayer and, I would claim, a new kind of praying, the language of what happens when flow-through meets go-across.

I read recently of someone's near- or after-death experience. His consciousness went all the way past the galaxies to the source of the source of light and asked a question of THAT. Which religion do you prefer on earth? The answer was a great relief. *I don't care.* Well, of course. So the Khajou Bridge is an excursion, an evening by the river, a poem of *unaffiliated* joy. Certain bridges are cathedrals for wandering and wasting time. Khajou is a jewel of the mystical imagination, full of secret ways for making the way home home. We need no railings here, no police, and nothing is being hawked. It's chancy, and subliminal.

Rumi has long been felt to be a bridge, a place for cultures and religions especially to merge and enjoy each other. During his ride with his

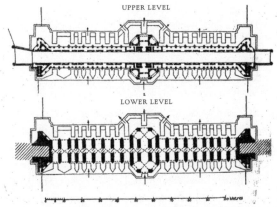

The spiral line through the center of the lower level is the view through the vaults

The floor plan of the Khajou Bridge.

family down the Silk Road ahead of the Mongol armies, from Balkh in central Asia to Iconium (Konya, Turkey), he accumulated a rich baggage of Taoist, Buddhist, and Zoroastrian images, along with stories from India, to add to those from his Islamic texts. It is said that ninety camels were needed just to carry Bahauddin's (Rumi's father's) books. There is a caravan bridge to contemplate.

Thoughts upon Silence

Rumi devotes a lot of attention to silence, especially at the end of poems, where he gives the words back into the silence they came from (*khamush* in Persian). It is truly one of the mysteries that flow through him. No other poet pays such homage to silence. He was once asked, "Isn't it strange that you *talk* so much about silence?" He answered, "The radiant one inside me has never said a word."

Here are some closing lines from this collection that include the silence after the poem as an integral part of the poem. They function as bridge links from the poem to the reader's consciousness following the poem.

Now let silence speak.
As that begins, we will start out.

#5, LEAVES ABOUT TO LET GO

Now the kissing is over.
Fold your love in.
Hide it like pastry filling.

Whisper within with
a shy girl's tenderness.

#9, THE TIME OF DIVULGING

Music begins.
Your silence,
deepen that.

Were you to put words with this
we would not survive the song.

#18, MUSIC AND SILENCE

Enough words. Friend,
you can make the ear see.

Speak the rest of this poem
in that language.

#19, EARSIGHT

Be silent now.
Say fewer and fewer praise poems.
Let yourself become living poetry.

#28, SOUL HOUSES

I will shorten this poem,
because the rest of it
is being said in the world
within our eyes.

Do you know this silence?
It is not the same as in your room
when you have no one to talk to.

This is pure silence,
not the kind that happens
when living dogs are eating a dead one.

#32, PURE SILENCE

Be clear like a mirror
reflecting nothing.

Be clean of pictures and the worry
that comes with images.

Gaze into what is not ashamed
or afraid of any truth.

Contain all human faces in your own
without any judgment of them.

Be pure emptiness.
What is inside that? you ask.
Silence is all I can say.

Lovers have some secrets
that they keep.

#38, NO EXPECTATIONS

The last ghazal above provides a list of the qualities of this silence that
Rumi serves. A clarity with no reflecting, no imagery, a courage that can
acknowledge any truth or shame, infinitely multiple identities, no judg-
ment, emptiness, and inside the emptiness secrets that will never be held
in language.

   More closing lines:

It is necessary for you
to experience nonbeing.

Love takes you toward that.
Asleep beside the splashing water,
let it say secrets into you.

Be a sleep and a pure listening
at the same time.

#45, ASLEEP AND LISTENING

Your love has brought us to this silence,
where the only obligation
is to walk slowly through a meadow
and look.

#52, THE ONLY OBLIGATION

A wealth you cannot imagine
flows through you.

Do not consider what strangers say.
Be secluded in your secret heart-house,
that bowl of silence.

Talking, no matter how humble-seeming,
is really a kind of bragging.

Let silence be the art
you practice.

#54, I SEE THE FACE

We grow quiet. Our souls become
one another and Shams Tabriz.

#60, GONE FOR GOOD

The love-ocean roils with praise,
and that sound increases now
as I end this and wait
for your discourse to begin.

#64, FAINT LAMENT OF FORM

I want these words to stop.
Calm the chattering mind, my soul.

No more camel's milk.
I want silent water to drink,
and the majesty of a clear waking.

#71, I ASK ONE MORE THING

Now a silence unweaves
the shroud of words
we have woven.

#82, ONE THING I DID WRONG

A northern wind arrives
that burnishes grief
and opens the sky.

The soul wants to walk out
in that cleansing air
and not come back.

The soul is a stranger
trying to find a home
somewhere that is not a where.
Why keep grazing on why?

Good falcon soul, you have flown
around foraging long enough.

Swing back now toward
the emperor's whistling.

#83, A NORTHERN WIND

Rumi's ghazals end in many different ways: bewildered, bereft, ecstatic, resigned, winsome, lost. Over five hundred close with this mention of silence. Sometimes it is felt as a waiting for a new way of speaking to begin, one that transmits the teachings that can come only in silence. And always Rumi is altering the tradition of mentioning the poet's own name, or pen name (takhallus), at the end as a way of signing the poem. He never does that, that I know of. He never *claims* the poem as his.

Another, much longer category would be that of poems that end with a turning toward Shams, sunlight, or the sunrise (Shams means "sun") or with observing some phenomenon that happens at dawn, as when most of the stars disappear and the planets brighten for a moment.

These words may not be pure truth,
but they contain an energy
that you can spend.

When the sun comes up, have you noticed
how some individual stars, by which
I mean human beings, begin to brighten?

#81, ENERGY YOU CAN SPEND

The wild presence of Shams Tabriz, Rumi's teacher and friend, can make deep changes in the human psyche. Rumi's poems offer the mystery of that presence to those listening, and with it a transformation as gentle and profound as that of the sun's coming up on a sleeping town.

The noise of a waking town
fills my chest. Shams
is saying this.

#90, A WAKING TOWN

So perhaps the hidden subject of this collection, and the hidden purpose of the Khajou Bridge, is to give form to our longing for silence and to the listening we do within that. Nothing can be *done* about such longing. This silence cannot be achieved through effort or practices, and having an intellectual understanding of silence is certainly not worth anyone's time. We must experience it, *be* it, be changed. It is a relaxation that surprises us in the evening. A dissolving of time and space, of you and me, into one timeless consciousness. It is the beauty that Rumi's poems swim, what they give a taste of. It has other names, this silence. Love, freedom, enlightenment. A flotilla of ducklings paddling sixteen watercourses.

TRAVEL NOTES

In May 2006, Robert Bly and I visited Iran. This escapade began with a phone call from Moe, Mohammed Mohanna, an Iranian businessman who builds skyscrapers in Sacramento. He had been talking with Ayatollah Zanjani, the recently appointed chancellor of the University of Tehran. Zanjani knows of the current popularity of Rumi in America, and he particularly liked my collection *The Book of Love.* He had suggested that the University of Tehran award me an honorary doctorate. I was open to that, though I never thought the idea had any chance of making it through the academic committees, since I do not work from the Farsi. My collaborative versions of Rumi have no status in the scholarly world. But the process kept moving along, and when it became a definite offer, I realized that it would be much more interesting to have a companion along.

I proposed that the university honor Robert Bly for his lifetime of poetry and poetry translation. Bly's work is already well known in Iran. University administrators said they were willing to award Robert a *plaque of appreciation.* So here was my predicament. Robert is my mentor. He *introduced* me to Rumi in 1976. When I was first publishing my poetry in 1968, he was winning the National Book Award. It was not right for me to be given the doctorate and him a *plaque.* I could not do it. I threw a tantrum, but it did not work. They had never given *two* doctorates at a

The Ayatollah, Coleman, and Robert in robes.

ceremony like this. I told Robert of my dilemma. He thought the whole thing was pretty funny, and he was game for the adventure. There was a wonderful moment in the green room before the ceremony when we were putting on our robes. They carefully explained to Robert that he would have to give his blue robe and hat *back,* but that I got to keep my carefully tailored black one with the gold trim and the silver wings, like Captain America's. He gave me a wacky, tongue-out-the-side-of-the-mouth look. I love Robert Bly.

I had inklings of what was going on in Iran before I went, ghastly news items from the Web. Robert was more knowledgeable, and our mutual friend, Andrew Dick, knew a whole lot about it. Andrew kept telling us, *"Don't go. Don't."* Up until the last day he was urging us to say we had food poisoning, appendicitis, jury duty, anything. He was afraid for us. Iranian intellectuals who speak against the regime *have* disappeared, it is true. Sufi centers have been destroyed, and many Sufis murdered. I still don't know what the actual danger was to us, if any. I have many Iranian friends. I hope that my acceptance of a doctorate from the University of Tehran does not imply support of the regime now in power in Iran. I am

told by those who have lived under it that terrible atrocities and execu-
tions have been performed over the last twenty-eight years by this group
that is so supported and controlled by the mullahs and ayatollahs. I wish
that there could somehow be a peaceful transition to a more democratic
form of rule, but I wish that for this country too. What we have here
in the United States is a global power conglomerate pretending to be a
democratically elected government.

Robert and I chose not to answer the political questions that were put
to us. What do you think of our president's letter to Bush? We deflected
those by saying we were on a literary pilgrimage. Our reticence was not
entirely natural. It was actually an agreement with one of the Iranian
Americans who arranged the trip. He had previously taken several inter-
faith delegations to Iran, and he had plans for future trips. His relation-
ship with the State Department was fragile, so he hoped we would avoid
bad-mouthing Bush while we were over there. Mostly we did avoid
doing that, until the last television interview, when Robert suggested to
the host that we arrange a trade. "We especially enjoyed Isphahan," said
Robert. *"If you will give us Isphahan, we will give you TEXAS!"*

A Sweet Morning in Shiraz

The first morning in Shiraz, as we are heading out in the van rented
for us by the University of Tehran to see the vast ruins of Persepolis,
Robert has a moment of sudden clarity. "No. Turn this van around. We
must go first to Hafez's tomb." A masterstroke. He tells me later that he
had a similar feeling of being about to make a mistake on his way to his
first marriage, but he did not act on that intuition then. Hence the tone of
urgency now.

We enter the peaceful sanctuary of Hafez's walled garden. At the gate
is a man with a box of cards with Hafez verses on them. A canary has
been trained to stand on the edge of the box and pick a verse at random
for each visitor. It is a response to a question, some advice for what one is
about to do, or commentary on one's life.

One line from mine says, "This lost wanderer has tasted his pure wine."

Robert and Coleman at Hafez's tomb.

One from Robert's says, "By night I sing, and at the hour of dawn I mourn."

We lounge against two pillars on the shady side of the high, magnificent cupola dome over the poet's tomb. Class after class, flock on flock of first, second, third, and fourth graders come through, making joyful clumps around Hafez's raised catafalque, singing.

Et O ces voix d'enfants chantant dans la cupole!

Robert calls them *little bits of Allah,* which is exactly what they are, the schoolchildren, so free and yet orderly too. Flecks of song. Both of us are weeping and laughing and writing in our notebooks. We read each other poems. It is a deeply beautiful morning.

Listen to this, Robert.

Totally conscious, and apropos of nothing,
you come to see me.

He writes the lines down. "These are published in a book, Robert."

"I know, but I like to see how they follow each other as I hear you say them."

Lo, I am with you always means when you look for God,
God is in the look of your eyes,

in the thought of looking, nearer to you than yourself
or things that have happened to you.
There is no need to go outside.
Be melting snow.
Wash yourself of yourself.

A white flower grows in the quietness.
Let your tongue become that flower.

Saadi's tomb is the second stop that morning in Shiraz. Close by there
are steps leading down to cool underground chambers with stone chan-
nels of swift-streaming, luminous springwater and a beautiful central fish-
pond with creamy gray fish. The place is full of boisterous high-school
students who want to crowd close and have their pictures taken with us.
Kneeling around the pool, we toss coins in and watch them wobble to
the coinage floor. The coins get nosed and inspected for possible nourish-
ment by the gray fish. No help there, they say. Such radiant arrangements
for a poet's grave. We Americans should have the imaginative generosity
to build such facilities around Walt Whitman's grave in Camden, Emily
Dickinson's in Amherst, Wallace Stevens's in Hartford. You can buy a

Coleman and Robert at Saadi's tomb.

great cup of sherbet at Hafez's place, and there is always music. We are not enjoying our poets enough. The Iranians have a lot to teach us about that.

There is a Saadi poem carved in Farsi on the wall just inside the door of the United Nations building in New York. It has no title in Persian, but it might be called "What It Is to Be Human":

Human beings come
from the same source.
We are one family.

If a part of the body hurts,
all parts contract with pain.

If you are not concerned
with another's suffering,
we shall not call you human.

SAADI

I was told of this magnificent poem by an Iranian taxi driver in Austin, Texas, Farid Mohammadi. He went with us to Iran and made a wonderful film of the journey.*

That afternoon we motor out into the thick heat and dust of Persepolis. "*Rockefeller Center art,*" says Robert, nailing every artifact ever funded and supervised by empire. No individuality allowed here. There is a fifty-yard-long bas-relief of emissaries arriving in procession with offerings from all over the world—Cappadocia, Tibet, Mongolia. Each looks like a standard cookie-cutter Persian, same beard, same profile. You may be a far, strange, unique being, but here you become another cog in the great Persian empire machine.

The Sex Police

One of the rules printed in a 1907 American pamphlet, *Guidelines for Female Schoolteachers,* is: Do not get into a carriage with any man

---

* Contact Farid on the Web at texasnafas.org for information.

except your father or brother. That 1907 rule is still being enforced in Tehran a century later, in 2007. A young man, twenty-two, heading to law school, told us of his friend who was riding in a car on a recent afternoon with a young woman his age. They were pulled over by the police and taken in, interrogated separately and at length, humiliated, and kept overnight. A man and woman are not allowed to ride in a car together if they are not married or are not brother and sister. Beware ye cousins and ye young lovers. People are careful what they say out in the street, in bookstores, almost anywhere, about this fundamentalist regime they live under. Conversation is more open in their homes, but still cautious.

The Women Students

Iran is a tremendously well-educated, deeply cultured society. I was told that maybe 80 percent of the people are not practicing Muslims. They seem mostly to try to ignore this government. They certainly do not want to go through another revolution. It has been twenty-eight years since the last one. There is no telling what you get at the other end of one of those things. I was also told by young people that there is not much hope this situation will change in their lifetime. When we spoke at Isphahan University, the crowd was overwhelmingly female, all in black with hair covered. You would not call them "coeds" under any circumstances. These are serious adults. Only 15 percent of these bright women will find jobs when they graduate. They asked challenging questions. "What makes you feel that you are able to communicate the

Bawa Muhaiyaddeen.

essence of what Rumi is saying?" I answer that my only credential for doing this work is that I met a true Sufi teacher, Bawa Muhaiyaddeen, in a dream on May 2, 1977, and that in some mysterious way he is helping with it. The revelation may have surprised them. I don't think many were satisfied about the question of my competence.

A college-age woman on the Western side of passport control in the airport told us with some passion that she was never coming back. "I have had it with those guys."

A Thunderstorm Supper

Tehran rises up a wide mountainside. The higher you go, the narrower and the more alpine the streets become. The restaurants there are spectacular and terraced. We had an alfresco meal there with a brilliant group of writers and professors. A spring thunderstorm ran us indoors or under partial shelter. The humor and depth of this gathering felt very European to me. Iranians are like goofy French intellectuals, and I mean that as the highest compliment. It would be absurd to ever go to war with these people, our brothers and sisters. But that, of course, is true of everyone. My teacher used to refer to humanity as "God's funny family." Tireless, endless diplomacy, please. Let us sit down to dinner, lamb, and listen to the rain.

A Few Things Americans May Not Know About Iran

Gas is fifteen cents a gallon.

There is no income tax and no sales tax, only a small real estate tax.

Tehran is a city of twelve million that does not seem to have any slums. Maybe there are some on the south side. We did not go there. It is mile after mile of twenty-story yuppie apartment buildings.

Shiraz has three million people. Isphahan has four million. That one city lost three hundred thousand men in the Iran-Iraq war.

Everyone drives a medium-size late-model car. All the men wear dark suits and no tie.

Eighty percent of the courses at the University of Tehran are taught in English. Can that be true?

The amazing traffic is more like a continuous concrete version of dirt-track stockcar racing in the southeastern United States. It takes unbelievable courage to participate in it. To make a left-hand turn is unthinkable. It is a chaos that somehow works, with very little, almost no, honking of horns. And Iranians do not seem to bother much about fender benders or filing insurance claims and all that. They just wave and keep going, what the hell. Most of their side mirrors are broken off.

If you are riding a motorcycle, you do not have to wear a helmet, and you can ride against the traffic, go on the sidewalk, through the markets, anywhere. Sometimes certain cars also go *against* the traffic for eccentric reasons I never understood.

Anti-American Feeling

There was very little anti-American antagonism. An American flag is hanging vertically in Tehran. As you get closer, you see that the white stripes are full of bombs falling. But there were no abrasive personal encounters. Iranians are extremely courteous with visitors, hospitality being the bedrock of their culture. Many small things reveal this. Every time the van would stop, not one of the five or six men traveling with us, no matter how inconvenient it was, would get back in the van until Robert and I climbed into our middle seat.

I am no student of history, so please forgive this next part, or skip over it. I have only the most cursory notion of what happened in 1953. But it seems to me that Iranians have good reason to be resentful and angry toward the United States. From recently released documents, I understand it is clear now that the United States, in that year, overthrew a democratically elected government in Iran and installed a dictator, the Shah. We did this because Mohammad Mossadegh, a tall, elegant, eloquent, beloved statesman with a European education decided, in 1951, to nationalize Iran's oil industry. He thought it appropriate that Iran own its *own* resources, for God's sake.

Throughout the 1920s, 1930s, and 1940s, oil profits went mostly to Great Britain. During that time Iran was getting about 16 percent of the money from the oil taken out of its home ground by the Anglo-Iranian Oil Company, which later became BP, British Petrol. Churchill wanted to invade Iran and take back the oil fields. Truman would have none of it. Then Eisenhower came to power and the CIA and the British MI6 conspired to arrange a coup. Kermit Roosevelt and Norman Schwarzkopf Sr., among others, were generously funded and sent secretly to Iran for the covert action. After it was successful and the Shah came to power, the profits were divvied up 50 percent to England, 40 percent to the United States, and 10 percent to Iran. With a storm of rigged propaganda and fake mob scenes Kermit Roosevelt and his CIA henchmen, along with the British Secret Service, managed to bring down this powerful world figure, Mohammad Mossadegh. He was on a *Time* magazine cover in 1951. Kermit got a medal. It was for fear of our installing the Shah again that students took hostages at the American Embassy in 1979.

This is my sense of what happened from the little reading I have done. Some facts and percentages may be off, but I hope the general outline is accurate. It was not to prevent a Communist takeover that we intervened in the Iranian governmental process. It was so that we and Great Britain could have the oil and two giant shares of the profits from it. We were arrogant and greedy and callous, to put it mildly. Three hundred people died in the firefights we instigated in Tehran. Mossadegh spent three years in solitary, followed by exile and house arrest in his hometown of Ahmad Abad until his death in 1967. The Shah allowed no expression of grief for this national hero. When the Islamic Republic came to power in 1979, the great rallying cry was against the era of American intervention in Iranian internal affairs. In 2000 Secretary of State Madeleine Albright apologized publicly to Iran, acknowledging in a speech the "significant role" that the United States had played in the coup against Mossadegh.

I am baffled as to why Robert and I did not run into anti-American sentiment. Surely it is there. Somehow in the exuberance of our celebration of their all-embracing poets, Rumi and Hafez, they did not bring up the lingering resentment they must feel for Americans. It was very kind of them. Robert likes to say that Rumi is a way for Americans to love Islam. It is also true that the current American enthusiasm for Rumi is a thing of wonder and delight to the Persian-speaking world. They respect us for that.

Scrapwood

One evening in Shiraz Robert and I take a walk with no cameras in attendance. We go along a side street talking of our fathers. An old man is sitting on the sidewalk ahead of us with a small foot-tall, foot-square table on which he is sawing a piece of scrapwood into kindling with a hacksaw. He sees us coming and puts table and saw aside. Holds open his arms to us, big smile. We stop at his storefront, where pieces of discarded wood are hanging by cords like skinny chickens. He has no language (a stroke perhaps), but he is obviously inviting us to sit down with him

Coleman and Robert talking.

and his work. He gestures to a bulletin board on the wall. Photos from younger days when he was charismatic and strong, resembling Meher Baba somewhat. We put our hands on our chests and bow to him. *But we do not sit down,* which is a mistake. When you meet the scrapwood man of Shiraz, the one beyond words, stay near, sit with him on the sidewalk, at least until he closes shop. Spend time with such givens. They are our true wealth: the Zanayeh River at Khajou, the voluminous, playful motions of Rumi's poetry, each other's splendid company.

Here are ninety poems for Rumi's 800th birthday. There ought to be ninety million, a galaxy cluster for this Milky Way presence that has gifted us with such friendship and spontaneity.

THE POEMS

A BOWL FALLEN FROM THE ROOF

You that give new life to this planet,
you that transcend logic, come. I am only
an arrow. Fill your bow with me and let fly.

Because of this love for you
my bowl has fallen from the roof.
Put down a ladder and collect the pieces, please.

People ask, But which roof is your roof?
I answer, Wherever the soul came from
and wherever it goes at night, my roof
is in that direction.

From wherever spring arrives to heal the ground,
from wherever searching rises in a human being.

The looking itself is a trace
of what we are looking for.

But we have been more like the man
who sits on his donkey
and asks the donkey where to go.

Be quiet now and wait.
It may be that the ocean one,
the one we desire so to move into and become,
desires us out here on land a little longer,
going our sundry roads to the shore.

A STORY THEY KNOW

It is time for us to join the line
of your madmen all chained together.
Time to be totally free, and estranged.

Time to give up our souls,
to set fire to structures and run out in the street.

Time to ferment. How else can we leave
the world-vat and go to the lip?
We must die to become true human beings.

We must turn completely upside down
like a comb in the top of a beautiful woman's hair.

Spread out your wings as a tree lifts in the orchard.
A seed scattered on the road,
a stone melting to wax, candle becoming moth.
On the chessboard a king is blessed again with his queen.

With our faces so close to the love mirror,
we must not breathe, but rather change
to a cleared place where a building was
and feel the treasure hiding in us.

With no beginning or end we live in lovers
as a story they know.

If you will be the key,
we will be tumblers in the lock.

HARVEST

As the sun goes down in its well,
lovers enter the seclusion of God.

Late at night we meet like thieves
who have stolen gold, our candlelit faces.

A pawn has become king.
We sit secretly inside the presence
like a Turk in a tent among the Hindus,
and yet we are traveling past a hundred watchmen,
night-faring, drowned in an ocean of longing.

Sometimes a body rises to the surface
like Joseph coming out of his well of abandonment
to be the clarity that divides Egypt's wheat fairly
and interprets the royal dreaming.

Some people say about human beings, *Dust to dust.*
But how can that be true of one
who changes road dust to doorway?

The crop appears to be one thing
when it is still in the field.

Then the transformation time comes,
and we see how it is: half chaff, half grain.

INHALE AUTUMN, LONG FOR SPRING

Union is a watery way.
In an eye, the point of light.
In the chest, the soul.

The place where ecstatic lovers go
is called the tavern, where everyone gambles,
and whoever loses has to live there.

So, my love, even if you are the pattern
of time's orderly passage, do not go,
or if you do, wear a disguise.

But do not cover your chest.
Stay open there.

Someone asks me, What is love?
Do not look for an explanation.

Dissolve into me, and you will know
when it calls. Respond.

Walk out as a lion, as a rose.
Inhale autumn, long for spring.

You that change the dull field,
who give conversation to damaged ears,
make dying alive, award guardianship
to the wandering mind,
you who erase the five senses at night,
who give eyes allure and a blood clot wisdom,
who give the lover heroic strength,

you who hear what Sanai said,
Lose your life, if you seek eternity.

The master who teaches us
is absolute light, not this visibility.

LEAVES ABOUT TO LET GO

This world of two gardens, both so beautiful.
This world, a street where a funeral is passing.

Let us rise together and leave *this world,*
as water goes bowing down itself to the sea.

From gardens to the gardener,
from grieving to a wedding feast.

We tremble like leaves about to let go.
There is no avoiding pain,
or feeling exiled, or the taste of dust.

But also we have a green-winged longing
for the sweetness of the friend.

These forms are evidence of what cannot be shown.
Here is how it is to go into that:
Rain that has been leaking into the house
decides to use the downspout.

The bent bowstring straining at our throats
releases and becomes the arrow.

Mice quivering in fear of the housecat
suddenly change to half-grown lion cubs,
afraid of nothing.

So let us begin the journey home,
with love and compassion for guides,
and grace protecting.

Let your soul turn into an empty mirror
that passionately wants to reflect Joseph.
Hand him your present.

Now let silence speak.
As that begins, we will start out.

A LIGHT WITHIN HIS LIGHT

I circled awhile with each of the intelligences,
the nine fathers that control the levels of spirit growth.

I revolved for years with the stars
through each astrological sign.

I disappeared into the kingdom of nearness.
I saw what I have seen, receiving nourishment
as a child lives in the womb.

Personalities are born once.
A mystic many times.

Wearing the body-robe, I have been busy
in the market, weighing and arguing prices.

Sometimes I have torn the robe off
with my own hands and thrown it away.

I have spent long nights in monasteries,
and I have slept with those who claim
to believe nothing on the porches of pagodas,
just traveling through.

When someone feels jealous,
I am inside the hurt and the need to possess.

When anyone is sick,
I feel feverish and dizzy.

I am cloud and rain being released,
then the meadow as it soaks in.

I wash the grains of mortality
from the cloth around a dervish.

I am the rose of eternity,
not made of water or fire,
not of the wandering wind
or even earth. I play with those.

I am not Shams of Tabriz,
but a light within his light.

If you see me, be careful.
Tell no one what you have seen.

A KING DRESSED AS A SERVANT

A sweet voice calls out,
The caravan from Egypt is here.
A hundred camels with amazing treasure.

Midnight, a candle and someone quietly waking me,
Your friend has come.

I spring out of my body, put a ladder to the roof,
and climb up to see if it is true.

Suddenly there is a world within this world,
ocean inside the water jar.

A king sitting with me dressed as a servant.
A garden in the chest of the gardener.

I see how love has *thoughts,*
and that these thoughts are circling
in conversation with majesty.

Let me keep opening this moment
like a dead body reviving.

Shams Tabriz saw the placeless one
and from that he made a place.

AS THE SKY DOES IN WATER

For the grace of the presence, be grateful.
Touch the cloth of the robe,
but do not pull it toward you,
or like an arrow it will leave the bow.

Images. Presence plays with form,
fleeing and hiding as the sky does in water,
now one place, now nowhere.

Imagination cannot contain the absolute.
These poems are elusive
because the presence is.

I love the rose that is not a rose,
but the second I try to speak it, any name
for God becomes *so-and-so,* and vanishes.

What you thought to draw lifts off the paper,
as what you love slips from your heart.

THE TIME OF DIVULGING

December is gone, along with January and February.
Spring is here. Tulip buds appear.

The empty trees stagger and flail
like drunks going home.

The wind recites a spell.
The rose arbor trembles.

The dark blue water lotus, *niluphar,*
says to the jasmine, Look how
twisted together we are.

Clover blossom to meadow grass,
This is the grace we have wanted.

The violets bow,
responding to the hyacinths,
and the narcissus winks,
An interesting development.

The willow slings her lightheaded
hair around, saying nothing,
and the cypress grows even more still.
Everybody is so beautifully
becoming themselves.

Artists go outdoors to let the beauty
move through their hands and their brushes.

Sweet-feathered birds light on the pulpit.
The soul sings, *Ya hu.* The dove
replies, *Coo, coo.*

The roses open their shirts.
It is not right to stay closed
when the time of divulging comes.

One rosebud remarks to the nightingale,
Lilies have hundreds of tongues,
but they do not tell their secrets.

No more holding back. Be reckless.
Tell your love to everybody.

And so the nightingale does.
The plane tree bends to the vine,
Stand up. The prostrating
part of prayer is over.

The vine, This prostration is not voluntary.
I have that in me that makes me always
like this, burning with surrender,
flat on my face.

It is the same power
that makes you *plane*.

The rose asks the saffron,
Why so pale?

The plump red apple replies,
Because saffron does not understand
that the beloved is absence
as well as this fullness.

Just then stones begin
bombarding him, but he laughs,
knowing how lover calls to lover.

Zuleikha tears Joseph's shirt,
but that is love-play to make him naked.

The apple absorbs a direct hit
and stays on the tree.

I hang here like Hallaj, feeling those lips
on me, the honor of being lifted up
on a crucifixion apple tree.

Now the kissing is over.
Fold your love in.
Hide it like pastry filling.

Whisper within with
a shy girl's tenderness.

EMPTY

Come out here where the roses have opened.
Let soul and world meet.

The sun has drawn a fine-tempered blade
of light. We may as well surrender.

Laugh at the ugly arrogance you see.
Weep for those separated from the friend.

The city seethes with rumor.
Some madman has escaped the prison.

Or is a revolution beginning?
What day is it?

Is this when all we have done and been
will be publicly known?

With no thinking and no emotion,
with no ideas about the soul,
and no language,
these drums are saying how empty we are.

NICKNAMES

The one my soul is searching for
is not here. Where has he gone?

The one like a lit candle,
like a seat with roses growing around it.

Our eyes look for that one first,
but I do not see him today.

Say his name. If anyone here
has kissed his hand, give us your blessing.

I do not know whether to be more grateful
for the existence of his face
or for what is inside that.

There is no one like him in the world.
But if there is no form for that now,
how is it everything turns
with the motion of his love?

Say all the possible nicknames
for Shams Tabriz.

Do not hide anything from one
who wants only to be in his presence.

NEW BLOSSOMS

Sit near someone who has had the experience.
Sit under a tree with *new* blossoms.

Walking the section of the market
where chemists sell essences,
you will receive conflicting advice.

Go toward kindness.
If you are not sure where that is,
you will be drawn in by fakes.

They will take your money and sit you down
on their doorstep saying, I'll be right back.
But they have another door they leave by.

Do not dip your cup in a pot
just because it has reached the simmering point.

Not every reed is sugarcane.
Not every *under* has an *over*.

Not every eye can see.
Or it may be you cannot thread the needle
because it already has thread in it.

Your loving alertness is a lantern.
Keep it protected from wind
that makes it crazy.

Instead of that airy commotion
live in the water that gently cools
as it flows. Be a helpful friend,
and you will become a green tree
with always new fruit,
always deeper journeys into love.

SPLIT THE SACK

Why does the soul not fly
when it hears the call?

Why does a fish, gasping on land,
but near the water,
not move back into the sea?

What keeps us from joining the dance
the dust particles do?

Look at their subtle motions
in sunlight.

We are out of our cages
with our wings spread,
yet we do not lift off.

We keep collecting rocks and broken bits
of pottery like children
pretending they are merchants.

We should split the sack
of this culture
and stick our heads out.

Look around.
Leave your childhood.

Reach your right hand up
and take this book from the air.
You do know right from left, don't you?

A voice speaks to your clarity.
Move into the moment of your death.
Consider what you truly want.

Now call out commands yourself.
You are the king. Phrase your question,
and expect the grace of an answer.

ANY SPRIG OF AN HERB

Learned theologians do not teach love.
Love is nothing but gladness and kindness.

Ideas of right and wrong
operate in us until we die.
Love does not have those limits.

When you see a scowling face,
it is not a lover's.

A beginner in this way
knows nothing of any beginning.

Do not try to be a shepherd.
Become the flock.

Someone says, This is just a metaphor.
But that is not so.

It is as clear and direct
as a blind man stubbing his foot
against a stone jar.

The doorkeeper should be more careful,
says the blind man.

That pitcher is not in the doorway,
replies the doorkeeper.

The truth is, you do not know
where you are. A master of love
is the only sign we need.

There is no better sign
than someone stumbling around
among the waterpots looking for signs.

Every particle of love,
any sprig of an herb,
speaks of water.

Follow the tributaries.
Everything we say has water within it.

No need to explain this to a thirsty man.
He knows what to do.

SECRET PLACES

Lovers find secret places
inside this violent world
where they make transactions
with beauty.

Reason says, Nonsense.
I have walked and measured the walls here.
There are no places like that.

Love says, There are.

Reason sets up a market
and begins doing business.
Love has more hidden work.

Hallaj steps away from the pulpit
and climbs the stairs of the gallows.

Lovers feel a truth inside themselves
that rational people keep denying.

It is *reasonable* to say, Surrender
is just an idea that keeps people
from leading their lives.

Love responds, No. This *thinking*
is what is dangerous.

Using language obscures
what Shams came to give.

Every day the sun rises
out of low word-clouds
into burning silence.

DOORSILL

Ordeal. The time of testing is here.
Words like *fortitude* and *valor*
mean something among people again.

Old agreements weaken and break.
When the knife reaches bone,
your life must change.

Be glad the refining fire
is around you.

Laugh as you stand on this doorsill.
Out of your dry thorn opens a rose garden.

I point to you, because you give me
joy that cannot be said.

Heavy blows beat about my head.
I need your compassion.

Muhammad's warriors have come
from the Kaaba to help me in this fight.

My reason says, Be quiet.
What can you know?

I try to be silent,
but my weeping comes anyway.

Muhammad says, You did not throw
when you threw.

This I feel now in my body
is like an arrow suddenly
released to its moment.

FLIGHTPATHS

Today I see Muhammad ascend.
The friend is everywhere,
in every action.

Love, a lattice.
Body, fire.

I say, Show me the way.
You say, Put your head
under your feet.

That way you rise through the stars
and see a hundred other ways
to be with me.

There are as many as there are
flightpaths of prayer at dawn.

MUSIC AND SILENCE

Lovers, union is here,
the meeting we have wanted,
the fire, the joy.

Let sadness and any fear of death
leave the room.

The sun's glory comes back.
Wind shakes our bells.

We are counters in your hand
passing easily through.

Music begins.
Your silence,
deepen that.

Were you to put words with this
we would not survive the song.

EARSIGHT

Do you want the sweetness of food
or the sweetness of the one
who put sweetness in food?

There are amazing things in the ocean,
and there is one who *is* the ocean.

Think of a carpenter's alert comprehension
when he builds a house.

Now think of the one
who creates consciousness.

It takes skill to extract oil from a nut.
Now consider how sight lives in the eye.

There is a night full of the wildness
of wanting. Then dawn comes.
You take my hand in yours.

There are those who doubt
that this can happen.

They pour powdered gold into barley bins.
They follow donkeys to the barn.

Enough words. Friend,
you can make the ear *see.*

Speak the rest of this poem
in that language.

THE TALKING

I have come here
to lay my head at your feet,
to ask forgiveness,
to sit in the rose chair
and burn my thorns.

Whatever I thought to do,
when I am here with you, is nothing.

I come to weep.
There is no escape from grief.

Outwardly I am silent. Inwardly,
you know how I am screaming.

Make my face yours.
I will shorten this poem.
Read the rest inside me.

Poor silent lover,
you have no one to talk to?

But your thoughts keep surging through
like an army of firebrands.

Alone, every person stays quiet.
Nobody speaks to a closed door.

But you are convinced
that you have lost your best companion.

Maybe you are already in the pure world,
beyond this scroungy wanting
and the metabolizing of nature.
No doubt.

CURRENCY

There is a tree
and a fire that calls to me,
My darling.

For forty years I wander wilderness,
tasting manna and quail.

A ship on the ocean is a marvelous thing.
But I have been sailing this boat
of mine through dry desert.

Moses, my soul, my friend,
when you hold me, this body
is a walkingstick.

You throw it down,
it becomes a snake.

You are the boy Jesus,
and I am your clay bird.
Breathe on me.
Let me fly out of sight.

I am the column you lean against
that moans when you leave.

What cover do you draw over me now?
In one moment I am a stone,
then iron, pure fire.

Now a jangling scale flopping about
with nothing in it. Now poised
in balance showing weight and purchase.

Feeding on a certain pasture,
I am the pasture.

They are tasting me,
wolf, sheep, shepherd.

Matter is meant to move and change.
That currency reveals meaning.

Those who belong with me
know I am the value
these forms are tokens of.

WATER FROM THE WELL OF THE SOUL

This world-river has no water in it.
Come back, spring. Bring water
more fresh than Khidr or Elijah knew,
from the fountain that pulses
in the well of the soul.

Where water is, there bread arrives.
But not the reverse.
Water never comes from loaves.

You are the honored guest.
Do not weep like a beggar
for pieces of the world.

The river vanishes because of that desiring.
Swim out of your little pond.

Go where all the fish are Khidrs,
where there are no secondary causes.

That water rises in the date tree
and in the roses in your cheek.

When it flows toward you,
you will feel a deep contentment.

The nightwatchman shakes his rattle
as part of his fear.

You will not need him anymore.
Water itself guards the fish
that are in it.

ANOTHER INVITATION

My mouth, my entire body, laughs.
A rose is all rose.

My loving is here with you.
You come before dawn with a torch
and take me, but my soul remains
back there alone.

Issue another invitation.
Do not ask for one without the other.

If you do not go tonight
and bring my soul to me,
I will become a loud, disruptive noise,
and I will not be making it alone.

THE ONE WHO LEFT

Bring back the one who left.
Lure him with music
or any irresistible pretext.

If he says, I will be there in a little while,
that is part of his beguiling,
his art that can tie strands of water into knots
and make weavings of the wind.

Do not accept those.
Bring the presence.

Sit down within that and live inside
what is beyond physical beauty,
beyond the sun's extravagance
or the handsomeness of human beings.

Yemen has the most exquisite rubies,
but the one I want to see
coming through the door
is the one who lives *here.*

DISCIPLINES

Do not expect to be always happy on this way.
You have been caught by a lion, my dear.

The friend dumps plaster on your head.
Think of it as expensive perfume.

Inside you there is a monster
that must be tied up and whipped.

Watch the man beating a rug.
He is not mad at it.
He wants to loosen the layers of dirt.

Ego accumulations are not loosened
with one swat. Continual work
is necessary, disciplines.

In dreams, and even awake,
you will hear the beloved screaming at you.

A carpenter saws and chisels a piece of wood,
because he knows how he wants to use it.

Curing a hide, the tanner
rubs in acid and all manner of filth.
This makes a beautiful soft leather.

What does the half-finished hide know?
Every hard thing that happens
works on you like that.

Hurry, Shams. Come back
like the sun comes back
every day with new
and powerful secrets.

PIECES OF A BROKEN CUP

Give me again what you gave last night,
the huge cup.

I threw it down, and now it is dangerous
to walk barefooted in here.
People are wounding their feet.

I am not talking about glass,
or wine fermented in a vat.

I am up and down at once,
helpless and nowhere.

A fine hanging apple
in love with your stone,
the perfect throw that clips my stem.

Ask me who I am talking about.
Tell me who I am talking about.

Do not stand on the bank.
Jump in the river with me.

If you stay there, I will stay.
When you sit down to eat, I sit down.

I am the wandering drummer
who marches alone into the arena
with his drum wobbling crazily,
tied to the top of his lance.

You are happy to be leading me around.
We escape from existence together.

Why do we have to go back
and be silent like fish
pulled up out of the water?

SPILLED SPEECH

As everyone drifts off to sleep,
I am still staring at the stars.

Separation from you *does* have a cure.
There *is* a way inside the sealed room.

If you will not pour wine,
at least allow me half a mouthful
of leftover dregs.

Secretly I fill my sleeve with pearls.
When the love-police detain me,
let your moon come down
and hold me in its arms.

Officer, I know this man.
I will take him home.

Let my wandering end as the story does
of the Kurd who loses his camel.
Then the full moon comes out,
and he finds what he lost.

These rocks and earth forms
were originally sun-warmed water,
were they not?

Then the planet cooled
and settled to what we are now.

The blood in our bodies carries
a living luminous flow,
but watch when it spills out
and soaks into the ground.

That is how speech does,
overflowing from silence.

Silk on one side,
cheap, striped canvas on the other.

SOUL HOUSES

Who is this king
that forms another king out of the ground,
who for the sake of two beggars
makes himself a beggar?

Who is this with his hand out
saying, Please, give just a little,
so I can give you a kingdom.

He heals. He enlivens.
He tells the water to boil
and the steam to fade into air.

He makes this dying world eternal.
His greatest alchemy
is how he undoes the binding
that keeps love from breathing deep.
He loosens the chest.

With no tool he fashions where we live.
Do not grieve for your rusty, iron heart.
He will polish it to a steel mirror.

And as you are being lowered into the ground,
closed away from friends, don't cry.

He turns the ants and the snakes
into beautiful new companions.

Every second he changes cruelty
to loyal friendship.

Remember the proverb, *Eat the grapes.*
Do not keep talking about the garden.
Eat the grapes.

From a rough stone ledge
come a hundred marble fountains.

Out of unconditioned emptiness
comes this planet with all its qualities.

Lakewater over there.
Out of one huge NO
comes a chorus of yeses.

Rivers of light flow from human eyes,
and consider your ears, where language
alchemizes into amber.

He gives the soul a house,
then another and another.

He descends into dirt
and makes it majesty.

Be silent now.
Say fewer and fewer praise poems.
Let yourself become living poetry.

THE WAVE OF THAT AGREEMENT

Every second a voice of love
comes from every side.
Who needs to go sightseeing?

We came from a majesty,
and we go back there.

Load up.
What is this place?

Muhammad leads our caravan.
It is lucky to start out
in such a fresh breeze.

Like ocean birds, human beings
come out of the ocean.
Do not expect to live inland.

We hear a surging inside our chests,
an agreement we made in eternity.

The wave of that agreement rolled in
and caulked the body's boat.

Another wave will smash us.
Then the meeting we have wanted will occur.

CALM IN THE MIDST OF LIGHTNING

When the love-lion wants to drink our blood,
we let him. Every moment we offer up
a new soul. Someone comes to collect
the turban and the shoes.

Calm in the midst of lightning
stands the cause of lightning.

The way I look is so fragile,
yet here in my hand
is an assurance of eternity.

A snake drags along looking for the ocean.
What would it do with it?

If, for penance, you crush grapes,
you may as well drink the wine.

You imagine that the old sufis
had dark sediment in their cups.
It does not matter what you think.

The flower that does not smile
at the branch withers.

Shams Tabriz rises as the sun.
It is night now.
What's the point of counting stars?

AVALANCHE

Poet, rake the strings. Strike fire.
Staying quiet is not for now.
Be generous.

A baby must cry before the mother
nurses. Make a noise, poet.

Want the deep friendship
out loud.

Dilate this love. Mention the name
of the one who started this.

What am I saying? Shams is Jesus
walking a mountain road.

I am a slow, bewildered
avalanche moving along somehow
trying to follow him.

PURE SILENCE

I have come this time
to burn my thorns,
to purify my life,
to take up service again
in the garden.

I come weeping to these waters
to rise free of passion and belief.

Look at my face. These tears
are traces of you.

I will shorten this poem,
because the rest of it
is being said in the world
within our eyes.

Do you know this silence?
It is not the same as in your room
when you have no one to talk to.

This is pure silence,
not the kind that happens
when living dogs are eating a dead one.

WHAT FEAR OF LOSS

When we are with you, what fear of loss
could we possibly have?

You change every grief to gold.
You give us the key
to each world we come to.

You sweeten the lips of those we love,
and you open their mouths in desire.

You are beyond all guessing,
yet within each guess.

Hidden, yet beginning
to be revealed.

We have fallen into the sugar shaker.
We are the ground beneath you.
Let someone else describe the sky.

Hold us in silence.
Do not throw us back
into some discussion.

A MOUNTAIN NEST

Have you seen a fish dissatisfied
with the ocean? Have you seen a lover?

Have you seen an image
that tries to avoid the engraver?
Have you seen a word emptied of meaning?

You need no name.
You are the ocean.
I am held in your sway.

Fire in your presence
turns to a rosebush.

When I am outside of you,
life is torment.

Then Solomon walks back into Jerusalem,
and a thousand lanterns illuminate.

The divine glory settles
into a mountain nest.

The emperor and the source of light,
Shams Tabriz, lives here,
with no location in my chest.

MILES OF RIVERSIDE CANEBED

The news has come,
but you have not heard.

Jealousy has changed to love.
Do you have any love left?

The moon has opened its face
and its wings made of light.

Borrow eyes to see this,
if yours cannot.

Night and day an arrow comes toward you
from a hidden bow.

If you have no shield
and nowhere to hide from the death
that is always coming closer,
you may as well yield.

The copper of your being
has already been transmuted to gold
by Moses' alchemy, and yet you fumble
in a moneybag for coins.

You have within you an Egypt,
miles of riverside canebed,
the source of all sweetness,
yet you worry whether candy will come
from a store outside yourself.

External form, you reach for shapes,
yet *you* are the Joseph.

Close your eyes, and gaze in the mirror,
at the flame that lit your senses.

Your body is a camel going swift
and straight to the Kaaba.

You think you are idling around town
on a donkey, or heading off
the opposite way, but you are not.

This caravan is a triumph
being drawn directly into God's reality.

SOLOMON AND THE WIND OF SPEAKING

Solomon is here. Prepare the house.
No need to mention the soul
when the soul within soul is present.

I was wandering without love.
Then love entered.

I was a mountain. I became straw
for the king's horse. No matter what
the king's country, Turkey or Turkestan,
I am his servant, close as soul is
to body. But the body cannot see
the soul as I behold the king.

Drop the load you have been carrying.
This is a lucky time, my friends.
Do not wait. Leap up, and ask
the hoopoe the way to Solomon's throne.
Say all your secrets and desires.

Your speech is a thousand distracting
winds, but Solomon gathers those
into a flock, a listening shape.

Solomon knows the language of birds,
and he controls the wind of speaking.

A MIXED-BREED APPLE

A little mixed-breed apple,
half red, half yellow,
tells this story.

A lover and beloved get separated.
Their being apart was one thing,
but they have opposite responses.

The lover feels pain and grows pale.
The beloved flushes and feels proud.

I am a thorn next to my master's rose.
We seem to be two, but we are not.

NO EXPECTATIONS

A spirit that lives in this world
and does not wear the shirt of love,
such an existence is a deep disgrace.

Be foolishly in love,
because love is all there is.

There is no way into presence
except through a love exchange.

If someone asks, But what *is* love?
answer, Dissolving the will.

True freedom comes to those
who have escaped the questions
of freewill and fate.

Love is an emperor.
The two worlds play across him.
He barely notices their tumbling game.

Love and lover live in eternity.
Other desires are substitutes
for that way of being.

How long do you lay embracing a corpse?
Love rather the soul, which cannot be held.

Anything born in spring dies in the fall,
but love is not seasonal.

With wine pressed from grapes,
expect a hangover.

But this love path has no expectations.
You are uneasy riding the body?
Dismount. Travel lighter.
Wings will be given.

Be clear like a mirror
reflecting nothing.

Be clean of pictures and the worry
that comes with images.

Gaze into what is not ashamed
or afraid of any truth.

Contain all human faces in your own
without any judgment of them.

Be pure emptiness.
What is inside *that*? you ask.
Silence is all I can say.

Lovers have some secrets
that they keep.

MOUNTAINTOP TROUGH

We are here like profligates,
three camels with muzzles
plunged in provender.

Other camels rage
with their lips stuck out,
foaming, but they remain
down below in the valley.

This windy mountaintop trough
is ours. It sustains and protects,
and you do not arrive here
by just straining your neck
to *look* at the mountain.

You must start out and continue on.
You have to leave the place
where everyone worries about rank and money,
where dogs bark and stay home.

Up here it is music and poetry
and the divine wind.

Be the date tree that gave fruit
to Mary, the *Let-it-be* of her heart.

Say a small poem.
Love the exchange.

An autumn willow has no fruit,
so how could it dance
in the wind of *Do-not-fear*?

It rattles and talks
with nothing to offer.

Give voice to a poem.
Let it end with praise for the sun
and the friend within the sun.

WHAT YOU GAVE

Why are you lying in the middle of the road?

From the love-wine you poured.

I may be excessive with my giveaway impulses,
but I still have what you gave
when you held my head against your chest.

You pour what you pour
without a flask, without a cup.

That mastery and generosity
washes away all restraint.

Reason burst just for the joy of it
when you gave me the bowl.

Something flows from your eyes
that is beyond a thousand false desires.

YOUR TURN AT DICE

As the sun sinks below the edge,
the senses close.

As the sun is with shadows,
as the heart takes form in a body,
then rules it, as man is born of woman,
so there is a secret inside your loving,
a horseman cloaked in a dust cloud
that he himself has raised.

This is not a chess problem to concentrate on
and solve. Trust, as when it is your turn
at dice. Throw the elements here down.
Read what has been given you.

There is a sun-warmth inside
nurturing the fruit of your being.
Shams is the name of that.

HOLIDAY WITHOUT LIMITS

Going into battle, we carry no shield.
Playing in concert, unaware
of the beat or the melody.

We have become grains in the ground underfoot,
fold on fold, layers of love, nothing else.

Obliterated, as when the eye medicine
is no longer even a powder.
Then it cures sight.

An accident gradually gets accepted
as the thing that needed to happen.
Sickness melts into health.

There is nothing worse than staying congealed.
Let your liver dissolve into blood.
Let your heart break into such tiny pieces
it cannot be found.

The moon orb wanes.
Then for three days you could say
that there is no moon.

That is the moon that has drawn
so close to the sun,
it is nowhere, and everywhere.

Send us someone who can sing music
for the soul, though we know
such longing cannot rise from a lute
or a tambourine, not from the sun,
or Venus, or any star.

As day comes, give back
the night-fantasy things you stole.
Admit your arrogance as the stars do at dawn.

When the sun goes down, Venus begins bragging,
claiming light, arguing her loveliness
over the moon's. Jupiter lifts a gold coin
from his bag. Mars shows his blade
to Saturn. Mercury sits on a high throne
and gives himself successive titles.

That is how it goes in the middle
of the night. Then dawn. Jupiter
is suddenly poor. Mars and Saturn
have no plans. Venus and the moon
run away, broken and terrified.

Then the sun within the sun enters,
and this night-and-day talk
seems a meaningless convention,
the lighting business.

A true holy day for a man or a woman
is the one when they bring themselves
as the sacrifice.

When Shams shone his light from nowhere,
I felt a holiday without limits begin
where once was just a person.

OUTDOORS AND THE PASSION OF THE GRASS

From now on the nightingales
will sing of us sitting here outdoors,
where wind lifts the hair of the willow
and starts her dancing.
God knows what they say
to each other then.

The plane tree holds out
its broad hands in praise of the meadow,
understanding just a little
of the passion of the grass.

I ask the rose, Where did you get such skin?
She laughs. How could she answer?

She is drunk, but not enough
to say secrets, not so dissolute as I am.

Wander with drunks if you want to know
what they have been hiding.

They will open the purse-mouth
and spill the lavishness.

There is a wine fermenting
in the breast of a mystic,
and a voice there inviting
you to a banquet.

A human breast can give milk,
but also wine, and also
there is a flowing there
that tells stories.

Listen as you take in the milk,
then the wine, and then the stories.

Lay down your cap and your cloak.
Start talking from the majesty itself.

And now be quiet.
Very few will hear.

Most copper does not change to gold
for any philosopher's stone.

Bring your words to Shams.
Let sunlight mix with language
and be the world.

A PREPOSTEROUS GUESS

Friend, you change what I lost
to a surprise gift.

You open my mouth in desire
and hand me the key.

A strange, preposterous guess
seems righter and righter.

I let other fictions go.
I am the contents of your seed bag.
Scatter me over the ground.

Let me be quiet
in the middle of this noise.

ASLEEP AND LISTENING

Day before yesterday,
fire whispered to the fragrant smoke,

Aloes wood loves me,
because I know how to untie it
and let it loose.

This burning must occur,
or nothing will happen.

Sperm cell disappears into egg.
Then a new beauty appears.

Bread and broth must dissolve
in the stomach before energy comes.
Raw ore gets refined into coins.

It is necessary for you
to experience nonbeing.

Love takes you toward that.
Asleep beside the splashing water,
let it say secrets into you.

Be a sleep and a pure listening
at the same time.

PEARL

What kind of pearl are you
that other birds love to fly
in the air of?

There is nothing in this world
that is not a gift from you.

Every king wants to be checkmated
by your rook.

I will not run away or flinch
from however you raise your arm to strike.

Just to be in your presence
is the point of my life, cooked
and drowned, nothinged, nowhere.

Someone who has not dissolved
still loves places.

But you say, Leave.
There is no place for you.

Remember Nizami? *You are my king,*
but I will not survive your reign.

GREEN WRIT

From behind a thin cloth
a blaze of straw pretends to be the moon.

There are those who destroy soul growth
by using sacred symbols in their talk.

When you fall in love with clothing,
it is like you ride a donkey
into deep mud and sit there.

Even a dog sniffs greasy bread before eating.
Have you ever seen lions
fighting over a piece of bread?
Why are you drawn to a beautiful corpse?

You are a continuous question about soul.
When the answer comes in,
the question changes,

the way a kindness in grape juice
turns it to wine, the way you
were born into this life.

Fire lightens and rises.
You bow when you hear truth.

Fall thieves the garden barren.
Then a spring justice knocks on the door.

You read the green writ
removing all restraint.

LOOK AT A FOUNTAIN

Those with no energy have gone.
You that remain, do you know
who you are? How many?

Can you look at a fountain and become water?
Can you recognize the great self
and so enjoy your individual selves?

Do you run from joy?
Perhaps the lion
should not flee the fox.

Let your loving and your soul
burn up in this candle.
Let a new life come.

The friend is at the door.
You are the lock his key fits.

You are a piece of candy,
the choice words of a poem,

the friend and the swallow
of silence here at the end.

DESOLATION

From the left and from the right
come vilification and blame,
but you stay filled with compassion.

The moon gives light so generously
that the dogs bay at it.
They do not affect the moon.

They are like critics, each
with a certain specialty.

A lover is a mountain,
not flecks of dead grass blown about.

A lover is a flock of gnats
alive and lost inside the wind.

If it is true that rules rise from love,
it is also true that lovers
pay no attention to rules.

Desolation everywhere is true cultivation.
Ignoring benefits is a benefit
in love.

Jesus calls from the fourth heaven,
where communion is celebrated,

Welcome. Wash your hands and face.
It is time to sit at the table together.

THE DANCE OF YOUR HIDDEN LIFE

Move your hair in the light.
Let it scatter amber,
as the souls of sufis begin
to dance, sun, moon, and stars,
around us in a circle.

We are dancing their dance.
A slight melody
enters the great wheel
and helps it turn.

A spring breeze makes everyone laugh.
Autumn wakes from his dead sleep.

Rose and thorn pair up.
Many people are dancing with snakes.

The orchard king from his secret center
says, Welcome to your hidden life.

They move together,
the cypress and the bud of the lily,
the willow and the flowering judas.

Ladders have been set up
around the garden,
so that everyone's eyes lift.

A songbird sits on a branch
like the kind man who guards the treasury,
and has just been paid from it.

Shoots emerge from a dark core.
The new leaves are tongues.

The fruit, our growing,
collective heart.

As they begin to form,
these apples, peaches, pears, and plums,
we understand what our tongues
have been doing.

LET THE SOUP SIMMER

As the air of April
holds a rosebush,
I draw you to myself.

But why mention roses?
You are the whole, the soul,
the spirit, the speaker,
and what follows *Say,*
the quarry and the bowstring
pulled to the ear.

The lion turns to the deer,
Why are you running in my wake?

There are thousands of levels
from what lives in the soil
to humanity, but I have brought you along
from town to town.

I will not leave you somewhere
on the side of the road.

Let the soup simmer
with the lid on.
Be quiet.

There is a lion cub
hidden in the deer body.

You are the polo ball.
With my mallet I make you run.
Then I track you.

THE ONLY OBLIGATION

Today a new madness
is trying to set us free,
tearing open our sacks.

Some nameless Bedouin
has bought Joseph again
for eighteen coins.

A narcissus sprouts through the ground.
Our souls, having pastured all night
on jasmine, leap up for the dawn.

The world is new, and you
have been chosen to say this poem,
because you are the one with the love bites on you.

Your love has brought us to this silence,
where the only obligation
is to walk slowly through a meadow
and look.

53

BUTCHER AND SHEEP

Do not despair when the beloved sends you away.
Today's rejection may turn
tomorrow to an invitation.

If the door shuts, do not go away.
Be patient, even if every possibility seems closed.
The friend has secret ways known to no one else.

Is it not the case
that when a butcher kills a sheep,
he does not leave the carcass?

Rather, he bends down and works more closely.
The sheep's life becomes the butcher's life.

The meaning with this is: There is
a great generosity in being killed by the beloved.
Solomon's kingdom goes into a single ant.

Both worlds combine in one heart.
I have traveled everywhere
and found no likeness for the friend.
Have you found one?

This silence gives a taste.
Whatever wine the friend serves
comes when language ends.

96

I SEE THE FACE

I see the face
that was my home.

My loving says, I will let go
of everything for that.

My soul begins to keep rhythm
as if music is playing.

My reason says, What do you call
this cypress-energy that straightens
what was bent double?

All things change in this presence.
Armenians and Turks no longer know
which is which.

Soul keeps unfolding inward.
The body leaves the body.

A wealth you cannot imagine
flows through you.

Do not consider what strangers say.
Be secluded in your secret heart-house,
that bowl of silence.

Talking, no matter how humble-seeming,
is really a kind of bragging.

Let silence be the art
you practice.

THE MEETING

When the friend opens the door and says,
You are here, please come in.
It is such a pleasure to give up talking
and listen to his long story
about Khidr, the guide of souls.

A tailor cuts cloth uniquely for each person.
Springs open in the center of the lake.
Trees move in the breeze that comes before dawn.

A nightingale sits in the rosebush and asks,
Who do you love? Tell me.
No one else is here.

The rose, So long as you are you,
I cannot. This is the passionate demand,
the one the burning bush made of Moses.

I am a sacred pool. Take off your shoes.
Wade in. You are the essence
of place and placelessness, honored one.
Take my hand.

The needle's eye will not accept
a strand of thread that is folded double.

So it is with you.
You find yourself holding the royal bowl
and welcoming all to the banquet.

The sun stands in fire up to its chin
so we can have daylight.

When you take the hand of someone you love,
what happens to those hands?

Your darling comes, and you ask,
How can I help? Come here.

Reason wonders, Should I go?
And your loving, Should I run?

The one you love signals,
Yes. I want both of you.

The table is there. Sit down.
Choose the bright company.
Do not worry about food.

Now I pass to you this silence,
so that the alternations of night and day
with their flaming language
may finish the story.

THE LIVING DOUBLENESS

I ask my heart, Why do you keep looking
for the delights of love?

I hear the answer back, Why will you not
join me in this companionship?

This is the conversation of being
a human being, the living doubleness.

Cool and in motion like water,
placed and passionate like fire.

Subtle as wind, yet obvious
as a wineglass poured to the brim,
spilled over and drunk down
all at once for a toast.

Like rain, you make any image
more vivid. Like a mirror,
you can be trusted to hold beauty.

There are mean people who see only
meanness reflected in you,
but they are wrong.

You are pure soul
and made of the ground.

You are eyeshadow,
and the kindness in eyelight.

A ruby from no telling which mine,
let yourself be set in a seal ring.

Lift the sword-discernment
that rules a thousand compassions.

Shams in the lovely shape of Shams,
spring source of invisible meaning.

THE VALUE OF THIS MOMENT

Morning wind, and the feel
of your face close.

A fragrance come from China
through western Turkestan to here.
Is there word of Shams?

I am dressed with friendship.
Your voice says in my chest
the value of this moment,
partridge cry on the mountainside,
a human eye, what people say
in praise of sunlight and nightsky,
of Joseph's face and Jesus' healing
breath, a walking cypress shadow,
a field in spring, firelight.

Shams is all these and a guide,
the hand that never pulls away.

OCEAN LIGHT

The moon at dawn stooped like a hawk
and took me and flew across the sky.

Traveling inside that light, so close,
my body turned to spirit.

I saw nothing but light.
The secret of revelation came clear
with my ship submerged in that.

As it moved, consciousness rose into being,
and the voice of consciousness
made every foam fleck a new bodying.

Matter receives a signal
from the sea it floats in.

But without the sun,
without the majesty of Shams,
no one would see the moon
or ever dissolve in ocean light.

LIKE A FIG

Who turns bitterness to love? Who changes
the poisonous snake around your neck to pearls?

The kind king who makes a demon a sweetheart,
who changes funeral to feast and blindness
from birth to world-beholding sight.

Who pulls the thorn from your palm
and puts a pillow of roses under your head.

For one, he kindles fire.
For another, the flames blossom
to eglantine around the head.

The same that lights the stars helps those
who cannot help anyone anymore.

What used to be thought of as sin
scatters off like December leaves
and disappears, completely forgiven.

Amen, says *who-is-it,* the joy
of inside and out. Like a fig,
this presence is all tasty.

A rapture that is physical strength
in the hand and the foot
and *reality* for the soul.

I send my love out now to ride the sunlight
and take this account of Shams to those
waiting faithfully at home in Tabriz.

GONE FOR GOOD

I have stumbled over buried treasure again.
What I thought came first comes last.

How shall we celebrate?
Do not expect your heart to return.

When it dissolves in love,
it is gone for good.

Fire-messengers come running.
All troubles begin here.

There is no sleep left in me,
nor any eyesight.

It is possible my head is a pumpkin
full of red wine.

I sit at table tasting bread and salt.
It is myself I taste.

I dip a jar in the ocean.
Filled containers become seawater.

At the evening prayer time
I go to see a friend
who looks out an upstairs window,
then comes down.

We grow quiet. Our souls become
one another and Shams Tabriz.

TWO LOVINGS

Soul comes wearing a shape,
with fragrance, with the new green,
with a trembling hand, with generosity.
No, that implies a being apart.

Companion and confessor at once,
red and yellow, you join me
in the gathering, and you stay away.

You come late.
You are the source of two lovings,
fire one day, ice another.

TALKING TO THE LUCK-BIRD

Your jasmine body shrugs a signal to me.
My soul flies against the constraining cage.

Now the luck-bird's shadow is overhead.
I shout, Go away. You are not part of this.

Oh really? says the bird of good and bad
circumstances. You refuse happiness?
You anticipate no troubles?

These wittering worries and wishes
keep human beings apart from the friend.

I want the face itself. As I say that,
the luck-bird goes wild for jasmine.

Now the fortune-teller and the enlightened
teacher, the body and the soul,
are as crazed as I am.

ALIVE WITH SCRIPTURE

Every moment a voice comes out of the sky,
a verse, Creation is ample
and full of grace.
Sura 51:47

Those who hear this in the soul respond,
They turn to God. They praise.
They bow down all the way with gratitude.
Sura 9:112

To the lord of ladders
by which the spirit ascends.
Sura 70:4

The carpenter of the imagination has no way
to make such a ladder. Only the one
who says, All are returning.
Sura 21:93

But the patient adze blade can help.
To receive what is given, be diligent.
Sura 28:80

Watch someone working with an adze.
Dissolve in that steady work.
Do not jump to some expected outcome,
saying, We will surely win.
Sura 26:44

Stay stubborn, as the adze blade
nicks hardwood. If you move up two rungs,
the people on the right will claim you.

If you reach the roof, they will say,
Above the above, on the star highways.
Sura 51:10

Sufi of the world's community,
rise to the circle of Sura 37:165,
the blessed arranged in adoration.
Listen. Be so empty
that nothing but God is left.
Purify the learning
that keeps you from knowing.
Sura 59:13

Bow like *nun,* the twenty-fifth Arabic letter.
Like the gerund sound *-ing* at the end
of a word, lie flat. Become soul-writ,
Sura 68, which begins with *nun,*
so alive with scripture that you stand
for those who have no hypocrisy.

Root like a lotus, plunging deep in the mud,
that does not mind a death-wind in its leaves.
Wait, for I am waiting too.
Sura 52:30

Study the orchard of some soul
that has lost the power
to grow anything.
Sura 68:20

That stays in its disastrous sleep,
morning black as midnight.
Sura 68:19

FAINT LAMENT OF FORM

Friend, I am a mirror
holding all six directions,
but I cannot contain you.

You shine here because
you polished the surface.
The sun once asked your sun,
When will I see you?

As you set, I rise,
was the answer.

This is not reasonable.
Reason cannot walk
where this poem is going.

The great splendor of intellectual clarity
becomes a grain of corn in love's bag,
waiting to be thrown out
around the fowler's snare.

You are the bird that plunges
into the ocean of mystery,
and that ocean becomes your turning center.

The joy of questions becomes a thousand
answering earring bells.

All day we revolve around your tree
like limb shadows.

Night comes, a weary sleep.
Then again at dawn the faint lament of form.

With you the body's dog-soul
becomes a fox.

Because of you a lion bows down
before a jackal.

More and more concentric skies appear
with the earth as their center.

You call for us to start out, and we do.
This is the journey Adam left paradise on.

The love-ocean roils with praise,
and that sound increases now
as I end this and wait
for your discourse to begin.

THIS HIGH MEADOW

I break out laughing. I frown.
I yell and scream. Sometimes,
if one jokes and giggles,
one causes war.

So I hide how tickled I am.
Tears well up in my eyes.

My body is a large city.
Much grieving in one sector.
I live in another part.

Lakewater.
Something on fire over here.

I am sour when you are sour,
sweet when you are sweet.

You are my face and my back.
Only through you can I know
this back-scratching pleasure.

Now people the likes of you and I
come clapping, inventing dances,
climbing into this high meadow.

I am a spoiled parrot who eats only candy.
I have no interest in bitter food.

Some have been given harsh knowledge. Not I.
Some are lame and jerking along.
I am smooth and glidingly quick.

Their road is full of washed-out places
and long inclines. Mine is
royally level, effortless.

The huge Jerusalem mosque stands inside me,
and women full of light.

Laughter leaps out.
It is the nature of the rose to laugh.
It cannot help but laugh.

Lilies and roses open inside me. I hear voices.
Patience says, *Good news. Union happens.*
Gratitude says, *I have made some fortunate investments.*

Reason says, *I feel sick.*
Spirit: *I have a sacred pearl.*
The pearl itself says, *I am near the wall's foundation.*

Ignorance: *I have nothing.*
Knowledge: *I own the whole bazaar.*

Abstinence: *I begin to understand.*
Poverty says, *I have no hat and no need for a hat.*

When Shams comes back from Tabriz,
all this will be explained
by his presence.

GRANTED

What happens in the world,
what business is that of yours?

Two existences have merged in a single temple,
but where is your smiling image?

Granted, there are terrible famines
with no bread dipped in wine anywhere.

You control what is manifest and what is hidden.
Where is your warehouse of grain?

Granted, thorn, scorpion, and snake exist.
But where is your rose-petal bed,
your joy that is a deep rest?

Granted, human generosity has dried up,
but you could still give us
a pension and a silk robe.

Granted, the sun and moon go down daily
into hell, but not your light and your fire.

Granted, the jeweler has nothing to sell.
He stands by his empty stall.
You could rain down pearls, if you chose.

Granted, there is no mouth, nor any language,
but where is your surging impulse?

Come with me while the wine shop is still open.
We are dizzy with meeting each other.

Friend inside my chest and inside my hand,
find your coat and your turban,
if you have not gone senile.

Whores have stolen your hat and carried off
your clothes. Who will take care of you now?

A stranger blocks us.
You could be the arresting officer
in this matter, the judge, and the gallows
if that were your inclination.

Word-scatterer, hush this conversation.
Say instead silence to those who never talk.

SALADIN'S LEAVING

You decide to leave
and once more darken into iron.

You bring to this place rose and lily and eglantine.
Let no one ever say you work for the adversary.

You brighten where you are.
You hold us together.

Now you lay on your side
in the laughing love-play we have had.

You honor this dance
with gold-scattering sleeves, Saladin.

Like the moon you turn
a grainfield silver.

WHAT YOU HAVE DESPISED IN YOURSELF

They are here with us now,
those who saddle a new unbroken colt
every morning and ride the seven levels of sky,

who lay down at night
with the sun and moon for pillows.

Each of these fish has a Jonah inside.
They sweeten the bitter sea.
They shape-shift the mountains,
but with their actions neither bless nor curse.

They are more obvious,
and yet more secret than that.

Mix grains from the ground they walk
with streamwater. Put that salve
on your eyes and you will see

what you have despised in yourself
as a thorn opens into a rose.

WINTER OR SUMMER

The great river that turns the bend of the sky
is here. The mallet that when it strikes
the ball becomes ball and sky and ground
is here. Noah, who built the ark
with his carpenter's discernment,
is here with us now.

He hands you a bite to eat.
You become a healer.

Do you love winter or summer more?
You may have whichever you like,
winter for you, summer for me.

Rose and thorn are equal here.
One contracts into itself with a wound.
One opens out and luxuriates.

One jumps in water that turns to fire.
One walks into fire, and it is sweet basil.

Doubt becomes proof. A fallen angel
who did not see the human glory
gets born as a person, and vice versa.

Khidr distributes living water.
Animals rise from the dead.

Philosophers call this *the primal cause.*
Now this blesses those philosophers
with kindness. The whole of existence
is a mirror whose essence you are.

Breathe lightly, so it will not cloud.
Belief and disbelief do not matter.

Be ignorant here. Knowing and imagining
are always after something, like a blind man
going door to door and *not* asking
for salve to heal his own eyes.

These words would love to change your body
to soul. Fish do not worry
where the shore begins.

Someone not in the water, not a fish,
considers those boundaries.

Walk the lovers' road with truth
and humility. Those two will take
your hand and sit you down by Shams.

ABRAHAM AND ISAAC

The beloved arrives. My roof and door
become living tissue. Stay tonight.

I have business in the city.
If you leave, I will not survive.
Give me one night.

Many people are in my care. Their blood
is my ascending planet. I must follow that.
Taste my blood, I beg.

A rare offer. Do you know how it is
for those with me? To die
seventy times and seventy times
be born again.

The prophet Isaac is dust by the door.
Die. I will bring you back.

Do not flutter in my hand.
Do not wince at the knife blade.

Laugh as you are pulled from the garden
and plunged into powdered sugar.

You are Isaac. I am Abraham.
How could I hurt you? Love is a father.

The beloved leaves like a gust of wind.
Do not hurry, I call. Go slowly.

This is as slow as I can move.
No one has ever seen me when I hurry.

Be quiet now. The gray sky-horse is lame.
Flame reaches to the thicket.
Quieter. Save some for another day.

I ASK ONE MORE THING

Today pour the full cup.
Slap the wheel already spinning
so frantically.

This wine is invisible,
yes, but the effect is not.

I ask one more thing
from the love that has given us
this dear time talking together.

Lift the veil
from the face of the king.

Why open a rosewater shop
and keep the garden secret?

You have set the river flowing.
Now release the ducklings.

We are the first double-leaf sprout
two inches out of the ground.

We need rain, or we may not grow
more than this. Cynics on all sides say,
You look for what does not exist,
and saying that,
they steal laughter from the fool
and music from the lute player.

I want these words to stop.
Calm the chattering mind, my soul.

No more camel's milk.
I want silent water to drink
and the majesty of a clear waking.

SEEDS AND RAIN

The mystery of action: We are seeds.
You are rain. A dear stain,
our seed coverings decay.

You mix with what is inside,
and a toast to the new begins:

A divine blade, the keen edge
of *now*. Now rest, for the soul

slides over these eyes, as Shams
Tabriz covers Shams Tabriz.

ONE BEING INSIDE ALL

Lovers, it is time
for the taste of fire.

Let sadness and your fears of death
sit in the corner and sulk.

The sky itself reels with love.
There is one being inside
all of us, one peace.

Poet, let every word tremble its wind bell.
Saddle the horse with great anticipation.

Flute notes are calling us into friendship.
Begin again. Play the melody
all the way through this time.

Sun-presence floods over.
Quietness is an empty cup.

Accept that you
must hide your secret.

STRUCK TENT

I am the tent you set up,
then strike, quill pen you sharpen,
then bear down on and split,
flagstaff with the emblem upside down,
particle in window light, a galaxy.

I am all skin, yet soul as well.
Without you, I am a fake.
With, as real as the cool
spring ground warming.

You say, I keep my distance
to see what dance you will do
out in the air, little dust grain.

Why would the sun speak to one bit?
Friend, you destroy and you restore.

Do what must be done
to this love that has no fear
and no sense of being safe.

OPEN WINDOW

How would it be if you appeared
in this open window?

It would be as though my hands and feet
were suddenly untied,
and life was pouring back in.

I would say, I have not smiled
or laughed since you left.
Wine has had no effect.

And you would tease, Such melancholy.
It may be catching.

Then I would wrap my shroud around
and offer my neck to your blade.

Cure this headache permanently.
You are the soul light in my eyes.

Words drift out on the air.
Let the musicians play now.
The stringed instruments, the tambourine,
and the drum, since no reed flute
is here today.

FULL SUN

There is one who teaches the moon
and the evening star their beauty.

Muslims, I am so mingled with that
that no one can mingle with me.

I was born of this love,
so now I hang from this branch.

Shadows are always changing, fleeing.
I feel that fear.

There is no peace
except in full sun.

A voice says, Quick, the rope trick,
and, Where did the moth go?

When you hear that, coil the rope
and begin to climb.

Fly straight into the candle,
this burning so dear no coolness
can tempt us out of its flame.

I ROCKED MY OWN CHEST

Yesterday I sent a message
as clear and steady as a star.

You that turn stoniness
to gold, change me.

I showed you the longing
and rocked my own chest
like an infant to hush
it from crying.

Undo your breast.
Take me back to love's first place
where we were in union.

How much longer
do I have to wander apart?

I will be quiet now and patient,
waiting for you to turn and look.

YOU SHALL NOT SEE ME

You are rest for my soul,
a surprising joy for my bitterness.

Imagination has never imagined
what you give to me.

The sound of someone whistling in the street,
or asking questions. If that person
is bringing word from you,
those sounds are worth more
than all the world's poetry.

There is nothing I want but your presence.
In friendship, time dissolves.

Life is a cup. This connection
is pure wine. What else are cups for?

I used to have twenty thousand
different desires.

The unseen king said once on Sinai,
You shall not see me.

But even though he said that he was not,
I have filled the essence
of that *he* with my soul.

The Christian trinity, the Zoroastrian
light-dark, I absorb them all.

Though my body has not noticed,
union has begun to see a new way to be.

Grown old with grief and longing,
when someone says *Tabriz*,
I am young again.

A BEAUTIFUL WALK INSIDE YOU

Through this blood veil
the lover sees a beautiful walk.

Reason says, There are only six
directions: north, east, south, west,
up, and down. There is no way
out of those limits.

Love says, But I have
many times escaped.

Reason comes to a marketplace
and begins haggling prices.
Love wanders away with other
business to transact, something
to do with incomparable beauty.

There are secret things happening.
Hallaj listens to whispers
and walks off the speaker's
platform onto a scaffold.

Dreg-drinkers have love perceptions
that reasonable men fiercely deny.

They say, We cannot go barefooted
in that courtyard. There is nothing
but thorns through there.

Love answers, The thorns are inside you.
Be silent, and pull what hurts
out of your loving's foot.

Then you will see gardens
with secluded rose bowers,
and they will all be inside you.

Shams is the sun
obscured by this cloud of words.

Maybe he will burn the overcast off
and let love clear and brighten.

LEAVING

Every moment love arrives from all sides,
but no more sightseeing.

We are leaving for pure emptiness,
traveling with friends we once lived with,
beyond angels, beyond spirit,
to our home city of majesty.

Load up. Say good-bye
to this dusty place. A young luck
rides at the head of us.

Giving up the soul
is the main business of this caravan,
with the chosen one leading,
the one the moon came begging to.

A humble, delicate girl is following
the fragrance of his hair.

The moon splits open.
We move through, waterbirds rising
to look for another lake.

Or say we are living in a love-ocean,
where trust works to caulk our body-boat,
to make it last a little while,
until the inevitable shipwreck,
the total marriage, the death-union.

Dissolve in friendship,
like two drunkards fighting.

Do not look for justice here
in the jungle where your animal soul
gives you bad advice.

Drink enough wine so that you stop talking.
You are a lover, and love is a tavern
where no one makes much sense.

Even if the things you say are poems
as dense as sacks of Solomon's gold,
they become pointless.

ENERGY YOU CAN SPEND

I am a cup in your hand.
Look in my eyes, and you will see
that I am a cup shape
in a hand that has no body.

The earth is crowded with descendants
of Adam and Eve. They are all images
of this love that has no form,

who knows what the desert sandgrain
needs, and the ocean drop,
who every moment opens and closes
inside our heart.

Watch a donkey trainer training a donkey,
reining it in, then releasing,
giving it water and sweet barley,
so that when it hears the driver's voice,
or his whistle, its ears will go up,
its head will turn.

Love does the same with us.
Constraint, freedom.

We put our heads out through
the wooden cage bars, but the body
cannot follow. We say,
I guess my wings do not work.

There is a vision that is fire.
Look there.

I say this for the sake of those
who will live after us.

You are dry tinder.
This love does not postpone
its changeover to light.

It leads you on the secret ways
where reason is no help.

Muhammad's eyes are closed now in sleep.
Flute notes dwindle away.

These words may not be pure truth,
but they contain an energy
that you can spend.

When the sun comes up, have you noticed
how some individual stars, by which
I mean human beings, begin to brighten?

ONE THING I DID WRONG

The bird in the cage of my chest
flutters excitedly.

My mad camel pulls at its tether.
A lion looks out through my eyes
and sees quarry. The river rises.
Along the bank new grasses appear.
Dawn wind blows through the rose garden.

Love left, because of one thing
I did wrong. Now it returns.

Compassion curves back here,
and lightheartedness.

A blind man throws away his cane.
A baby begins to eat from the plate.
A falcon lifts toward the king's drum.

Now a silence unweaves
the shroud of words
we have woven.

A NORTHERN WIND

Every second the question comes,
How long will you stay dregs?
Rise. Do not keep stirring
the heavy sediment. Let
the murkiness settle.

Some torches, even when they burn
with spirit, give off more
smoke than light.

No matter how hard you stare
into muddy water, you will not
see the moon, or the sun.

A northern wind arrives
that burnishes grief
and opens the sky.

The soul wants to walk out
in that cleansing air
and not come back.

The soul is a stranger
trying to find a home
somewhere that is not a *where.*
Why keep grazing on *why*?

Good falcon soul, you have flown
around foraging long enough.

Swing back now toward
the emperor's whistling.

MIDNIGHT AND SUNRISE

This midnight restlessness
does not originate on earth.

No headache, no fever,
no black bile, no dropsy,
but it seems epidemic, this love.

No advice helps,
no cool restraint.

This intensity is invisible.
Have you seen love?
Or heard it?

There are no chants
to chant. Keep silent.
No theatrical magic.

Shams Tabriz is the source
that can melt this diseased and frozen world,
as now his healing splendor rises.

THE CREATION WORD

Three days now it has been like this.
I dip my pitcher in the fountain.
It fills with blood.

The rose garden is all desert
thorns and stone.

I chant spells to lure the genii back
into the bottle. Nothing happens.

A beloved's frown destroys the lover.
Come back. Brighten my eye,
even if I do not deserve it.

My loving asks, What have I done?
A voice replies, Do not look to yourself.
The cause is beyond every here and now.

The life gift is given
and then taken away.

It is not for us to know why, or how.
Grace comes with the creation word, Be.

That gate opens without hesitating.
Between the push of *buh*
and the smooth launch of *ee,*
there is an infinite moment
when everything happens.

86

WE ARE THE SUN

We are a warm spell
that comes in a relentless winter.

We are the sun with all the different
kinds of light. We are wind.

Doves, when they call *coo,*
where, are looking for us.

Nightingales and parrots change
their perches hoping to be nearer to us.

Word of us reached the fish.
They swerved and leapt.

Waves from that stirring keep coming in.
The soul has been given its own ears
to hear things mind does not understand.

In the great spirit world Muhammad's name
is called with his four friends,
Abu Bakr, Omar, Uthman, and Ali.

Those are our names too.
We have come out of slavery
with bales of sugarcane.
No need to mention Egypt.

The sweetness of how we talk together
is what we crush and bring the world.

YOU MAKE YOUR OWN OIL AS YOU COOK

Your kindness cannot be said.
You open doors in the sky.

You ease the heart and make
God's qualities visible.

We taste your honey and fly around
as happy as bumblebees.

You remember what was agreed upon
before the universe began.

You hear the sound of those praise-words,
Am I not (Yes!) your lord?

Poisonous people, you have little
to do with, only what is necessary.

You make your own oil as you cook,
beyond any recipe or idea of soul growth.

You look to meet another someone like
Shams Tabriz. You will not find that.

A HUNDRED AND ONE

Your life has been a mad gamble.
Make it more so. You have lost now
a hundred times running.
Roll the dice a hundred and one.

You have become a single string
stretched on the fret.
Expect to be struck.

Falcon's claw on the dove's soft side,
you cannot find your home again?
Hire a guide.

You have carved a pretend piece of wood.
This is my horse, you say.
Fine. Ride it to the next level.

You do not hear God talking to you?
You pray instead. That is prayer
without worship, brother.

You must bow completely down
to be beheaded.

Garlic and onion smell wonderful,
but try to catch the fragrance of amber.

When Shams accepts you as companion,
sit near him and listen.

WE CANNOT DECIDE

There has never been beauty like yours.
Your face, your eyes, your presence.

We cannot decide which we love most,
your gracefulness or your generosity.

I came with many knots in my heart,
like the magician's rope.

You undid them all at once.
I see now the splendor of the student
and that of the teacher's art.

Love and this body sit inside your presence,
one demolished, the other drunk.

We smile. We weep, tree limbs
turning sere, then light green.

Any power that comes through us is you.
Any wish. What does a rock know of April?

It is better to ask the flowery grass,
the jasmine, and the redbud branch.

A WAKING TOWN

The taste of this life comes from you,
soul moving like a mountain stream
under a sky of flowers.

Seeing such beauty makes me
expect the dregs tomorrow.

I call you *moon,* but that
is not right. Does anything
resemble you?

The noise of a waking town
fills my chest. Shams
is saying this.

References

Most references are indicated by a pound sign followed by the standard number of the ghazal in Professor Furuzanfar's eight-volume *Kulliyat-e Shams* (Tehran: Amir Kabir Press, 1957–66). Some of these translations have been done in collaboration with the translations of the Cambridge Islamicist A. J. Arberry in his *Mystical Poems of Rumi* (Persian Heritage Series No. 3, Chicago: University of Chicago Press, 1968) and *Mystical Poems of Rumi* (Persian Heritage Series No. 23, Boulder, CO: Westview Press, 1979).

Others were done in collaboration with Nevit Ergin's work. Since the 1950s he has been engaged in translating Rumi's *Divani Shamsi Tabriz* from Golpinarli's Turkish. The references here that begin with a numeral (and sometimes a letter, e.g., 8a, 7b) *not* preceded by a pound sign are to the particular volume in Nevit Ergin's twenty-two-volume translation, *Divan-i Kebir* (Echo Publications, 28 South Norfolk Street, San Mateo, CA, 94401; twenty-two volumes published between 1995 and 2003) and to the ghazal numbering (a pound sign with a number) within that particular volume. A project is under way to discover and list the corresponding standard Furuzanfar numbers for Dr. Ergin's work, but that task is not yet complete. See the Web site at www.dar-al-masnavi.org/erg-foruz-concord.htlm.

1: #100; 2: #1649; 3: #524; 4: #2737; 5: #1713; 6: #331; 7: #2730; 8: #900; 9: #581; 10: #330; 11: #1235; 12: #563; 13: #1353; 14: #498; 15: #132; 16: #984; 17: #19; 18: #34; 19: #605; 20: #743; 21: #1414; 22: #294; 23: #84; 24: #163; 25: #1139; 26: #1604; 27: #779; 28: #909; 29: #463; 30: 8a, #77; 31: #1156; 32:

#745; 33: #115; 34: #64; 35: #2828; 36: #58; 37: #968; 38: #455; 39: #1301; 40: #2845; 41: #943; 42: #2942; 43: #927; 44: #115; 45: #863; 46: #480; 47: 8a, #20; 48: #498; 49: #446; 50: #196; 51: #322; 52: #376; 53: #765; 54: #122; 55: #45; 56: #2760; 57: 8a, #82; 58: #649; 59: #528; 60: 7a, #86; 61: 3, #191; 62: 8b, #154; 63: 8a, #152; 64: #2170; 65: #2142; 66: #2144; 67: #2899; 68: 8a, #40; 69: 8a, #44; 70: #2092; 71: #10; 72: 8a, #37; 73: #34; 74: 5, #14; 75: #69; 76: #566; 77: #143; 78: #207; 79: #132; 80: #463; 81: #477; 82: #508; 83: #26; 84: #321; 85: #484; 86: 7a, #117; 87: 8b, #218; 88: 8a, #91; 89: 7a, #71; 90: 8b, #165.